Western Settings

Western Literature Series

WESTERN SETTINGS

Red Shuttleworth ⋆⋆⋆ *p o e m s*

▲▲ University of Nevada Press   Reno & Las Vegas

University of Nevada Press, Reno, Nevada 89557 USA

Copyright © 1975, 1976, 1986, 1990, 1997, 2000

by Red Shuttleworth

Manufactured in the United States of America

Design by Carrie House

Library of Congress Cataloging-in-Publication Data

Shuttleworth, Paul, 1944–

Western settings : poems / Red Shuttleworth.

p.   cm. — (Western literature series)

ISBN 0-87417-348-5 (pbk. : alk. paper)

1. Ranch life—West (U.S.)—Poetry.

2. West (U.S.)—Poetry.

I. Title.

PS3569.H865W4   2000   99-37039

811'.54—dc21   CIP

The paper used in this book meets the requirements
of American National Standard for Information
Sciences—Permanence of Paper for Printed Library
Materials, ANSI Z39.48-1984. Binding materials were
selected for strength and durability.

First Printing

09 08 07 06 05 04 03 02 01 00

5 4 3 2 1

To Kate

and

To Maura, Ciara,

Luke Appling, and Jessi

Contents

Acknowledgments

Much of the poetry in this collection first appeared in the following publications: *Calapooya, Calapooya Collage, Jeopardy, Kansas Quarterly, Mississippi Valley Review, Nebraska Review, Ontario Review, Pennsylvania Review, West Branch,* and *Yarrow.* Special thanks go to these magazines and their editors, especially Karl Patten and John Mann.

"Doc Holliday Recalls Meeting Kate Elder," now part of "Western Settings," originally appeared in *New Letters* (summer 1975). It is reprinted here with permission of *New Letters* and the Curators of the University of Missouri–Kansas City.

"A Widow's Grief," now #1 of "Western Settings," and "Frank James at Age Seventy, 1913," now #3 of "Western Settings," are reprinted from *Prairie Schooner* by permission of the University of Nebraska Press. Copyright © 1986 by the University of Nebraska Press.

The work in this collection was also represented in several of my chapbooks: *Sucking on Rattlesnake Bones* (Texas Portfolio Press, 1976); *Living and Sinning for Them* (Signpost Press, 1986); *Western Movie* (Signpost Press, 1990); *Coyotes with Wings* (Gorse Press, 1990); and *All These Bullets* (Logan House Press, 1997).

Without the abiding friendship and support of Whiskey, Lar, Hoss, and Dr. Des Moines, I might not have endured. We've had us some grand 'n western times. And mescal toasts to Jerry, Miss Julie, The Davey, and TGL for the gift of Nevada.

Western Settings

Old Night Friends

They aren't my coyotes. From our bedroom,
we listen each night as they teach
all the ways to live on mouse, stray cat,
or sick calf. There are no turning points,
just onward, full-tilt, feast-or-famine runs.

When my son was five, he believed
coyotes could make themselves invisible.
That way two or three could lie beside
his bed all night to give him sweet dreams.
He knew of one who ate cigarette butts.
Another had a paw taken from him
by God, punishment for hand-envy.
His favorite could sing along with Ian Tyson
while eating off lamb carcass.

When coyotes sing now,
usually off in the apple orchard,
I nearly ask my son to translate.
But he's sixteen. He'd tell me I'm
losing it. He has no recollection
of bedroom coyotes, not of the one
called Bloody Tongue who couldn't stop
brushing his teeth on locust thorn trees,
Bloody Tongue who nuzzled my son
during lightning and thunder,
who once snuck downstairs, took six
chocolate chip cookies off the table,
and shared them in bad weather.

Yeah, Hoss

I just made this up.
  —Waylon Jennings

1

After a leg of lamb and sweet-corn supper,
we sat near the corral with fisted Busch cans,
laughed about the thirty-cow breakout.
Okay, awful things are going to happen.
As we reckon it out, we are dumbfounded.
So what? I'll take the plump, unwashed puppy
in the ad. I'll bring the sick calf into the house.
With old clothes for a dog's bed, I'll let
the puppy dream the journey from littermates
to my couch. At midnight the puppy will nestle
against my heartbeat, my breath and calf
breath in its face. I once pictured my life
as the scarred river beside the cabin
the outlaws were blasted from.

2

During the Civil War, blinky-eyed Jesse James
set fire to Lawrence, Kansas. Zee had sent cake
along with the boys. Frank splits it in half
and hands his brother a share. Not a dozen
words pass between them as they potshot civilians.
Jesse smirks when Frank takes to quoting
Shakespeare to a man bleeding to death
in a burning buggy. Frank, the neater
brother, has finished his vanilla cake.
Jesse, who recently attended a wedding in El Dorado
Springs, has saved his portion of cake.
He wants to mash it lovingly upon the lips
of the prettiest Jayhawk widow he can find.
"Should we rob trains when this is over?"
Frank considers the question. "Why not?
Age is not a ripening." Generations pass,
and now we hear a train approach, smell
the nervous men in the baggage car:
five horsemen, grim with Winchesters,
are waiting. And we hear Waylon's voice,
"Come on, Jack, the son-of-a-gun's a-comin'."

A railroad crossing buckles and snaps
silently as I wake up alone. From the south
comes the smell of alfalfa burning three miles
off at the pellet plant. Half-eared cattle
call for me to fill the old stock tank.
I lose track of time and listen like a boy
waiting for Christmas morning. Kate shouts
from the kitchen downstairs, something
about calling the vet and going to town.
Toss me an apple, Woman, or hustle your
breasts back into bed. The business
of morning takes us too far from the joys
of nightfall: beer, guitar songs,
our children calling to screech owls.

Yesterday there were violet postcard clouds
and generations of sunlight on a photograph
of Cole Younger in his old age, the outlaw
filled with bemused forgiveness for the way
the Northfield bank robbery went down.
After all, he's on the county fair circuit
with Frank James, making money with grins.

While in prison, Cole Younger dreamed of running
in weightless boots. The heel of his right hand
was knife-scarred, and the palm of it was no longer
gun-calloused. He told his cellmate, "While Jesse
and Frank were riding stolen blind horses out of
Sioux Falls, I was a tourist attraction in Northfield.
Spurting blood from eleven bullet holes,
I sat beside my broke-legged horse,
itchy in woolen underwear, and tried to remember
all the decent whores I'd ever pleasured."

6

When I was a boy, I visited Wyatt Earp's
marble tombstone in the Jewish cemetery
in Colma, California. The one girl
who'd screw had a bruise-colored face.
Thanks to her drunkard stepfather.
I daydreamed a gazelle dinner
with an aging Hemingway, but he was
busy with Mayo Clinic shock treatments.

Now it is the month of mud-speckled ice,
stump heavy, and a man on the road
wants his skin bark-thick. Dusk names
all the women I've loved. Nothing melts
in this hour of pocket-hidden hands,
this whistling out of the cold Dakotas.
Lie down, lie down, an owl cries,
and I jog down the gravel road
to a circle of lamplight, to Kate
who hides chocolate kisses and bakes
black bread to the music of my knife
skinning cottontails. Lie down, lie down,
I tell our children, whispering names,
tucking in deer and raccoon blankets.

Think About It, Darlin'

1

A boy is lying flat in a patch of hemp
the sheriff is curious about, the constellations
of summer whirling. His chunky girl
considers the dumb age of him,
dips her fingers into a plastic
bag of stale candy. She wants to be the tan
goddess of barrel racing or a gunfighter's
woman in a sour-breathed epoch. She wants the boy
to wake up so they can make Wayne County Fair's
free dance. She wants to see just how drunk
his parents are going to get. The boy
touches the unloaded .44 Colt beside him
in a greasy, shot-up coyote hide.

2

Along with thirty other junior high
bag-lunchers more interested in the Giants,
I was one of the last people to see
Wyatt Earp's first gravestone. A month later
someone made off with all five hundred
marble pounds. The caretaker admitted that
down below was merely a jar
holding the ashes of a private life:
"He never really done all them things . . .
it's just stuff in them old books."
Some of it's true. Likely not enough.

3

What I intended was to complete the story
sixty-eight-year-old Bat Masterson was writing
when he died over a typewriter in his *New York
Telegraph* office. Damn it, I was only a boy
when I came to that intention. How was I
to know Masterson was reduced, often,
to combing the hair of the dead?
Before Bat's heart convulsed, he wrote,
"Not many of the West's ruined doves were beautiful,
but Squirrel Tooth Alice had a waist so small
you could tie a cowboy's sock around it,
and her skin was the color of the inside of an apple.
I loved the sound of her walk . . . something like
September corn stalks. She called me Bartholomew,
not Bat. I'd wake up with her auburn hair in my face
and the smell of her like vinegar pie. I'm a sports
writer now. If I need extra money for wagering fights,
I notch-up a pawn store .44 Smith & Wesson and sell it.
Doc Holliday and Luke Short are gone. Oh, I loved
Squirrel Tooth Alice in a large way, and I only asked
for one last staggering kiss when she and a porky
cattleman married in the Long Branch. He wasn't
terribly willing, but he reasoned well with
the barrel of my pistol holstered in his mouth."

4

The saloon music of our frontier
was an undertaker's dream.
John Wesley Hardin wrote
(he was practicing law in El Paso
and a week short of taking
a bullet in the back of his head),
"The notches on my six-shooter
are foul. What a woodpile of fools.
I never shot a decent man."
It's instructive to learn a man tanned
the hide off George "Big Nose" Parrot
and then got elected governor of Wyoming.
The governor arrived after the event,
but he talked often about Parrot's
bungled train holdup. The governor's
wife wore the Parrot-skin shoes
and stuffed the purse with cheap jewelry.

5

Along the way I lost a beaver skull
from a happy year in British Columbia.
We sank in house-deep snow, bought pears
in the world's coldest grocery store,
moaned and rolled all night in love.
We still have a moss-stained bear skull,
my show-and-tell from a moose hunt.
Now the world is sometimes peripheral,
a scar on my brain from the last wrecked car.
Rubbing or kissing skulls for luck probably
works for someone else. I prefer driving
to Lee & Rosie's Bar for a bottle of tequila.

My son stamps his boots at Kate, says,
"No, goddamnit, I ain't comin' inside."
Kate goes off mad. Jim and I keep drinking
in the corral. We watch Luke ride
a vanilla-colored dry ewe, one hand fisted
to a dog collar, the other hand raised
and flapping a gored Stetson. What will
remind Luke of love when he's my age?
Framed photos of black-'n-white rides?

7

A thousand or more bales are up
and a wall-cloud, shaped like
a horror movie atomic-mutant
butterfly, is bearing down on us.
Jim pulls two more beers from
the cooler as I piss on the corral.
I've got him half convinced
the way to handle the farm crisis
is not another Willie Nelson
Farm Aid Concert, that the way
is to drive a thousand longhorns
to the White House lawn
for serious grazing.
The only thing Jim thinks might
not work are horses . . . if the TV boys
send out helicopters for some
eyewitness news.

8

In Greenwood Springs for the dedication
of a new tombstone for Doc Holliday,
Bat Masterson limps to the waxed bar.
A woman called Rose is laughing.
"I near suffocated from his stink,"
she brags of Holliday. Masterson will write
it all down for the *New York Telegraph*,
having dumped being a shootist lawman.
He wonders if Rose really knew the dentist
with an anthracite heart, this Rose who is best
seen in a mirror by soft firelight.
Bat wonders if the roofers have finished
work on his Manhattan brownstone,
if his wife is still on a diet.
Doc's been dead for a waterfall of years.
God, he was a crusty skeleton of evil fever.

9

Finally drunk with dusk, I load
the feed bunk with alfalfa-colored pellets
and dull-yellow cracked corn, and hose up
the stock tank for the calves. Luke pops
his cap pistol and tells the poor goat,
"Goddamnit, I've had enough of you,"
and tries to mount up one more time.
Another ride on the dry ewe is
out of the question . . . she's been
rode to serious weight loss.
Jim walks off toward his black-as-a-
country-singer-tour-bus Jeep.
I brush away at a tick on my shirt,
admire its grip, its adolescent-like hope,
the way it crawls toward more life.

King of the Gunslingers

She kept telling me the weather
was a salty donkey, a bloody mary
—Willie Nelson—morning, a dog
left behind with the old folks.
The gunfighter's widow, heavenly-photo
child bride, was now sixty like a feral
nanny goat, not that anyone in heaven
was going to deny her that pleasure.

Bubbling with old grudges, "Well, sure . . .
some deserved dirt in the mouth,"
she bloomed teenager again
with her gunslinger's Colt. She told how
Johnny Ringo's brother played
major league baseball, "You can look
it up," and she said God spoke
Spanish to her in a quivering, deep growl.

It was almost summer, tree-planting time,
and her parents were speechless
when she brought him home to roost
back in the Second World War,
what with the groom being eighty.
He told the neighbors to bugger
each other, told the newspaper boy
to shut his trap or get kicked
all the way to Alcatraz, and he meant
to bake bread in his girl's oven.
"There's no death," she said,
"only rub-outs."

It Will Never Be Noon Again

1

I woke to the wolfhound's barking.
I'd been asleep with a chunk of gristly
hog in my mouth, with an eye-load
of flinty wolves running two-legged.
Sometimes I'm a marble slab or a black car
the size of a movie star's bed,
and every few yards my wheels
pop the heads of snakes. I stand,
look out the window. I shouldn't have called
her Snout. Now my daughter's sulking
by the barn door. I see a snake near
the granary and a lamb is drinking
from the wolfhound's bowl.
How in the hell am I
supposed to get through life
on the luck there is in petting
a poorly tanned squirrel hide?

2

Down in Texas it is November, and the yard
at Huntsville Prison is cold.
The warden's dog walks spider-legged,
and the warden's wife grabs the phone
as someone injects death into a killer's
well-muscled forearm. John Wesley Hardin
has been on parole a hundred years.
Hardin will not lead the choir tonight.
Someone else will have to make it Christian.
And this Nebraska is neck-scarred
by a sloppy noose. There's more
to be found in bankers' pockets
than badger teeth. I tell my guitar-picking
daughter to write a song about the time
Jesse James was brought lung-shot to Rulo
after the Civil War. As soon
as he could ride, Jesse rode.

3

We've been at this marriage for fifteen
photo albums. Somehow we've kept
the love of two sleepers
tangled in flannel sheets. I remember
a disused Pentecostal meeting hall
we lived in, the field mice in its walls,
the way Kate fried bread with bacon that winter
we almost gave up. Brooding, my chewing
tobacco tasted like wool. Shit, but we wake
up in odd rooms, thigh-to-thigh lovers,
our maps plum-stained, and the mountains
are holes at the folds. Kate sewed
curtains to mute the sun. We talked rattlesnake
meat and skipping out on each other.
Barren fields, locust thorn woods,
the eyes of shotgunned cottontails.
It all comes back like a badly addressed letter.
But it's morning, and we grin like kids
drinking beer. Our children parade
in tattered coats, cowboy scarves,
and cottonball beards. Love is the moon on fire.

4

Hell, I don't own any of it. Only that lamb
a local rancher calls my "lawn buffalo."
The thing to do about it all, he tells me,
is to buy a killer (a horse at auction
that'll be dog food), train it to stand
under gunfire, ride it into the First National
Bank of Winside, Nebraska, and ask for all
the loot, mortgage papers, and directions
to the place where the villains tied
the beautiful girl to the railroad tracks.

5

Meanwhile, I'm soaking a finger in hot water,
as if that's what you do when a piece of squirrel
claw is embedded in your own blood and pus.
Everything has its revenge, but my friends
keep spraying Agent Orange on their fields,
and I keep eating squirrel stew. With my good hand,
I flip on the radio. This is the cackle
and cracked voice of the Great Plains:
barbwire, ag loans, the weary target practice
a poor man takes with a secondhand Ruger .44.
These are what might be called rolling hills.
A place where back wheels slip on wet
high-crowned county roads. Just before
the ditch bounces up and turns the car over,
the children rub their hands together
for the warmth, for the loneliness
all hands feel. But it's nearly spring.

6

"Just think of it," the rancher says,
"it's biblical: you ride into that bank,
shoot it out and get shot. . . .
See . . . You'll have died
for everyone's sins."
Yeah, Hoss, me 'n Jesse James.
But I figure they want you to do it
with guitar and drugs from Nashville to Austin.
Yeah, I figure the locals want someone
to do their living and sinning for them.

Ernest Hemingway

Every wrinkle deepens. Rifles in middle age
sing there's no going back, not to the month
of fangs or the morning of sequins
on that girl south of Sun Valley whose father
scarred her breasts with winterkill
horse ribs. And the sky rains needles.
In middle age you can't remember
what you whispered to your babies.
You sing in Spanish as you slice onions,
and the voice belongs to autumn light
on packed snow. You punched the father
through his screen door, and the girl
bought sequins with your money.
And every stranger seems to have a letter
of introduction from Camus. If you could
go back to the fleshy hills where the cradle
of man offered no more than two plane
crashes in a row, the sunlight
might not remember you. That girl from
south of Sun Valley, the expensive shotgun,
the cruise across Nebraska in the convertible:
the sky is a blurry text, no more helpful
than ritual bedmaking. Stop crying.
There's no enemy here, and, yes, it's
bewildering that something's been won.

Just Before the Hot, Steamy Guts of June

1

The first sodbusters ate mutton and lashed
their children. I won't top that.
The wind is up. There's the clackety-
clank of the useless windmill. At least
I'm the kind of man who will go fool-naked
in October snow to get a woman's laugh.
All day long my daughters took snapshots
with four-dollar plastic cameras
that came with sunglasses. They took some
of me pouring cheap whiskey into the dog's bowl,
one of a slice of toasted barley bread
coated with almond paste, and another
of my boy riding a snowy dry ewe
for a perfect 100-point score.

2

Before he says his last words, Wyatt Earp,
dying of prostate cancer near an L.A. beach,
hears the muffled footsteps of his three children.
He is eighty-one, and the children are buried
in Abeline, Dodge City, and Tonopah,
their ages totaling less than a month.
Upright against the headboard, tilted away
from the weight of a Colt .45 holstered below
his left armpit, Earp listens to Josie phone
movie cowboy Tom Mix. Someone will have to
carry the coffin. Earp pours a small amount
of dirt from an envelope onto his tongue,
then draws and cocks the pistol
he thinks is loaded. He dry fires.
He mumbles, "Suppose . . . suppose . . . ,"
and dies with Mojave grit on his tongue.

3

I love the wooden look of the Great Plains
in old sepia photographs, clean and ready
for cattle in cloud-broken sunlight.
A Sunday passed spraying thistles
and mending barbwire fences,
I finger mulberries from a chipped bowl,
think about Lyndon Baines Johnson,
our president who lied about his great-
grandfather dying in the Alamo.

4

Hauling prairie hay, the first man who
lived on this place died beneath
a horse-drawn wagon. In another year
almost forgotten, a drunk hunter
bled to death in a tangle of barbwire
beneath the bridge I walk to at night
while the children eat ice cream.
The hours grope onward, and the windows rattle
in a thunderstorm. My boy is sleeping,
paired-up with an empty Jim Beam bottle,
a keepsake from the night a bronc rider
praised his sheep riding.

5

Lines from a diary:
Doc Holliday was the silent messenger,
a bullet's last inches. He died in light
the color of pus on a concave chest.
We buried his black dentist's bag,
his good-luck Wichita gutter stone,
and we burned his lip-red bedding.
A woman in the hotel's grease-pot kitchen
wept as if she knew Doc's gentlest touch.
We asked Doc what Earp was like, Masterson
and Ringo, too. But he stayed quiet
almost to the end. Then he smiled
and said, "When I stop to think
about it all, it's terribly funny."

6

The motion of it all is not sadness.
I won't mind growing old, not if
Bat Masterson was right:
"The last intimacies taste
of rainwater and Kentucky bourbon."
Masterson passed through Nebraska
more than once, but he thought it was better
to circle the state like a dog around an old blanket.
At worst the motion is comic, like the kids
scraping coyote grease off a hide,
telling Kate that's how makeup
is made for models in TEEN magazine.

A coyote follows the turn of a cottontail
beside the creek. I walk back to the house,
and my oldest daughter says her latest painting
is done: sky and a badger-shaped cloud.
If this was someone else's life,
meeting the inventor of the cattle prod
on a plane out of Sioux City would
have been a dream. The wolfhound chews
his rump, and my son tells me a ghost
lives in an upstairs closet. Kate folds
the caramel-colored bedspread. I give her
a beery kiss as the baby wakes from a nightmare,
and the oven burns a tray of chocolate chip cookies.
I own a schoolboy's love for strawberry perfume.

Western Settings

And our lives was like
Some old Western Movie.
   —Guy Clark, "Desperados Waiting for a Train"

1

Jesse James left behind a young wife.
On this 1897 afternoon, his widow
is beside herself, smelling, as she does,
meat rotting off tree-hung cow and hog skulls.
Her daughter intends to oil paint them
for Halloween. Widow James would like
to consult brother-in-law Frank,
but he is busy reading Shakespeare,
Francis Bacon, or is it Karl Marx?
Frank James paws his balding head:
"If there's ever another war in this country,
it'll be between capital and labor,
between greed and manhood. And I'm
as ready to march now in defense
of American manhood as I was
when a boy in defense of the South."
That's fine, thinks widow James,
but what about Mary James? Mary's
already painted three deer skulls:
one red, one blue, one white, all with
golden antlers, and Mary has named them
Jesse, Frank, and Cole Younger, and has
commissioned a brass plate for the town
library . . . "The Trinity of God."
And now there's that damned photographer
from the Kansas City paper, demanding
iced tea, praising Mary's mad trinity.
Widow James is trying awfully hard
not to scream, "If only your father
was still alive . . . "

2

The town's beauty queen is shoveling out
her uncle's barn. She's pretty like a hand-carved
pistol grip, like the Arabian mare she barrel races.
She bakes crusty bread, loves to herd cattle.
She's shoveling horse manure, and her cousin walks in,
a boy her age in saddle-worn jeans.
She picks an ant out of her curly auburn hair,
says, "I'm gonna have your baby." He tells her he
loves the sky best when there are violet storm clouds,
tells her about a bucking horse named Hog Killer,
but he doesn't tell her about the banker's daughter
singing in church, or about a certain grass-stained
yellow blouse. "Listen, boy," she says, "I got something
a little worse'n a wasp-stung hand." "You betcha," he says.

3   *Frank James at Age Seventy, 1913*

I loved my brother, but for years
I've been selling pebbles off Jesse's grave.
Ty Cobb came around one winter with a bottle
to warm us. He gave me a baseball, a new Colt,
and leatherbound volumes of Shakespeare.
I gave him a true stone, the others having
come from my nephew's farm. Teddy Roosevelt
came, too, but I charged him the regular
half-dollar admission and handed him
a gallstone an undertaker removed
from a vagrant, and I charged Teddy
twenty dollars. He really thought he
was special because of some Cuban hill
a horse managed to get him up. There he was
with the gallstone, the Yankee kneeling
over Jesse's pebbled grave, half listening
to how we'd near lost it all in Northfield.
One of his footmen dropped the gallstone
in an envelope: it's in the White House now.
My son finds my small business as irritating
as a chigger bite, thinks there's no dignity in it.
I say it's the spirit of the nation.

The Flat was a buffalo hide of a town.
They built a horse pen over a hundred feet
above Main Street with a long hall up to it.
A hundred dollars was offered to any girl
who'd jump, astride a white horse,
into a mammoth barrel of water. They found
a yellow-haired soiled dove, bought her
a lace petticoat, set the jump for a Saturday.
Hundreds drinking and watching, she led
a blinded horse up the elevated chute.
Bareback, fingers weaved to the horse's mane,
she yelled, "Pull the bolt, turn us loose to fly."
They streaked down like a flash of birch,
baptized us, then rose like sea gods atangled.
They called for a doctor as they pulled
her from horse and water. Blood
painted her mouth, chin, petticoat.
"Gimme my hundred . . . and a mirror,"
she screamed. I touched her broken nose.
"Am I still worth twenty a night?"
"Even more," I grinned as she heaved
her freckled breasts. "Good, then I'll come
with you tonight," she giggled, "and you can help
spend short fame and dollars in this town."
I took her birch-white thighs, by God,
took her on through until morning.

5

Doc Holliday tosses the sky's breastbone
into the campfire. He's on the way to Glenwood
Springs to die in a hotel. Doc kneels
by the fire, rubs his hands,
the purple light of the Rockies
all around, rustling like the skirt
of a woman he loved in Tombstone.
He will not live long enough to read
Bat Masterson on prizefighting, or
long enough to see Wyatt Earp subdivide
Los Angeles for a million more dollars
than Frank and Jesse took off trains.
Doc is pissed off because he wants to be.
He grabs the sky's fatty heart and bites it.

6

I wandered across another man's farmyard.
Breaking with the land, he called in
a tongue-clicking auctioneer to sell milk cans,
a gopher gasser, and short-legged cattle.
The priest was there, his plum-colored
Chrysler blocking traffic up the dusty lane.
The wife, hands knotted for weeks on the notion
of moving to town, faced it all from the roof
of her home. And the idiot son-in-law
pawed his haunches, lolled his tongue
at a bull-eyed blonde girl who aimed
a video camera at the crowd of neighbors.
Getting the hang of it, the need to smell
another man's ruined life, I bought
the gopher gasser for a goddamned buck.
The blonde arched her back sharply
as the son-in-law strained sideways,
thumbed her buttocks. Her freckled skin
went mean-red. She put him down
with a right to the nose, a left
to the mustard-stained "Dairy Farmers
Have Warm Hands" teeshirt.
By then the auctioneer was about hoarse,
begging us to bid on cracked railroad ties.
In that depth of shot dreams, there was
quiet disturbed only by a pheasant hen
suddenly wing-flapping off and the auctioneer
blowing his nose into torn Kleenex.
The priest left with a bag of bridge nails,
slamming his car door at the high prices.
The blonde left with her camera, three cans
of motor oil in a sack, and a small rabbit
drugged or dead in a cage. I would have

bought more, helped peel more bark
off the farmer's life, but I don't want
to become an expert, always picking
the best pieces off the bone,
a crow on a road kill.

7

Henry Starr is trying to rob
the two banks in Stroud, Oklahoma.
At the same tangled time.
It is 1915 and he'll never know
he should have waited ten years.
He could have done it in silent films.
He's a cougar, Belle Starr's nephew,
and he had the touch, but now
guns are going off and he won't
outlive his horse. It turned out
the same for Doolin and the Daltons.
Starr cannot stop nourishing
his adrenal glands. He carries
a pistol for the sound it makes.

8

The northbound flight of geese and a man
loading a Ruger .44 revolver. The rotted
granary roof quivers beneath the flapping
of black wings. Inside the blue farmhouse,
two girls drop coins into a cracked piggy bank.
Here is the sun on mute lilacs,
the same sun that leads us to senility.
Gunfighter Doc Holliday didn't even have
his trousers on when his lungs filled with
phlegm thicker than horse sweat. All these
bullets, separate as nuns, eager as Reynosa whores.
It's false summer, muggy and the color
of a silk blouse left on a tombstone.
The taste is of long-gone strawberries.

9

Dark-bearded and in need of a beery woman,
Doc rides salt flats. He's an eternity
from pass the popcorn. Somewhere in Valdosta,
a cousin waits for her period. If it comes,
she will become a nun. But that was before
Doc bought his first Colt .44 and before
the woman called Big Nose. His white shirt
smells cheesy from a tubercle. The sun
comes at him in waves like a season of incest.
Back in Denver, they'll remember Doc Holliday,
oh yes, every time the pistol-whipped policeman
strolls into a saloon. Doc throws away
a toothpick and knows he will soon be
that light. If he is already dead,
this is certainly a most curious dream.
If the boy pouring him a last whiskey
in Glenwood Springs is a memory,
then this riding is a tune the devil
got fooled on. Doc turns his head as if
his shadow ahorseback could be seen.

10

Mouth open wide in the ride of sleep,
My son rolls against his stuffed bear.
The storm has smoothed out like ironed
dollar bills for a birthday, its lightning
only a momentary glaze over South Dakota.
I brace myself with a shot of whiskey,
walk up the fenceline. One of my steers
takes me for who knows what and bursts
bucking into the pasture's windy center.
Leaves are turning. Suddenly I feel
like I can eat a whole bag of frozen
strawberries or a pound of chocolate.
I want to wake my daughters who believe
there's an owl princess who wears earrings
and a gown of milkweed floss. Suddenly
I laugh remembering the afternoon my son
poured a bottle of cologne on a calf.
We're the kind of family that will stand
on the front porch in the middle of
the night to applaud a full moon.

Looking for Belle Starr

The Rodeo Queen Special was $3.49:
raspberry ice cream between buttermilk
waffles topped with Comanche cherries.
The motel bartender, over a whiskey ditch,
said, "Love's like neon . . . it always
tells a joke." Yeah, I bought
the teeshirt for a friend: magenta
mountains and a motion-picture horseman.

Years ago another friend left her parents'
bathtub naked, bloody wrists and black lipstick,
and stumbled four miles across Galveston.
"I'm an eclipse of the moon," she said,
"a lesson in controlled fire." For love
she'd done her best in a gooseneck on straw.

It was the Fourth of July in Alma, Nebraska,
like drunks dog-paddling the Republican.
Belle, you weren't at the motel
junk-food machine after closing time,
a cross between Miss July and the hatchet
face you were: storebought fragrance
of citrus and branding iron.

Journey

1974

Stuffed, it'll have all the poise
of a woman who has worked
toward a long agony. The dead
wolf's hair is frozen to the blood-
glue floor of the luggage compartment.
The bus is only ten minutes late
into the congealed town of Chetwynd, B.C.
It took that long for everyone
on the bus to have a look
at what the driver went over the yellow line
to hit so perfectly that only
the neck's busted.

1975

The night wind off the Mojave
tastes of your tangerine mouth.
The miles shift between hawks.
Kate, you taught me, more than
any woman, the glide of a summer hand
over apricot skin is everything until
no breath is left. My hands
must never become arithmetic in texts.
Here in this Barstow motel, a portrait
of a lady is on the wall, done with rose
petals stuck together with moonlit
pinesap. If I shout, Regret and Longing,
a hawk will carry the words to you
wherever you love. I'm learning
to help when I can.

1980

A day short of being thirty-six,
I locate another fatty tumor on the wolfhound.
Tomorrow, a time of presents I've seen already:
a mended jacket, framed snapshots of my girls,
a bottle of Power's Irish whiskey. A day
of applecake, Sunday newspapers, a quiet
walk with the old dog. Killing chickens today
with a friend, we talked of cobblers and Brueghel.
It is the middle of a simple life lost from
baseball. I carry a pen and notebook,
consider the milkweed by the lake, wonder if
Wyatt Earp truly shot a tumor off his dog's leg.
A day short of being thirty-six, I run three miles
to feel the inflamed chest cartilage, to feel
how my knees hurt. My countrymen build saloons,
churches, war planes. My countrymen, let's bring
back the cobbler, the grizzly, girls who wear
plaid shirts in redwood forests. Whiskey-breathed,
I sing with Kate and Bran, "Good Ole Boys Like Me,"
sing Hank Jr. and Waylon, sing the moldering
color of October prairie. I'm just a day short.

1983

It is the silence of alfalfa round bales
in late December, snowdrifts holding them
like so many thighs. I unscrew the thermos lid
and pour canned pears into your mouth,
so warm in this 30-below-zero hour.
Southbound clouds blot out the moon.
The nearby road is icy black, forming a gravity
of its own. You ask, "Is this a good month
to cook road kills?" Roast raccoon,
boiled carrots, and Irish tea to pass the night.
In the midst of this, we once again try
to dump the ashes of Pup, the old wolfhound,
and once more decide there is too much wind.
This is not the right darkness for letting go.

1986

Hours to bread and juice, and it's weeping
a blizzard. Pine branches dip low.
A coyote runs belly-close-to-ground
in a roadside ditch. Fence wire disappears
in blowing snow and comes back glossy with ice.
All around, and it's nearly dawn, the sky
descends in daughter-like tenderness.
Sleepless, I stumble boot-heavy into my barn
and startle a possum. There's no place
to lie down . . . drunk one night I spread
mouse traps in the oddest spots.
A pair of dogies are in separate stalls,
in a panic for dead momma cows.
I pull an apple from my coat pocket,
tongue the skin. In a land made for horsemen,
something is snapping its fingers in a grave
below winter wheat: a knotted music for lost love.

1987

I'd even buy firecrackers in the rain for you.
You drop off the porch as if in a ballet, lope naked
into the dusky farmyard, pink from your shower,
bend to pick up the pliers I left by the goat pen
in the bromegrass, turn your milky breasts to me,
and I fall in love again. Maybe I ought to notice
there's a tip of sun in the last evening cloud,
and maybe I ought to do something about our corn garden
getting grasshoppered to shreds,
but my heart is flackering like barn pigeons
after a shotgun blast. Hell, I know
I ought to pay attention to the coyotes
who chewed up over a hundred pounds of geese
last night, or pray for the friend who
drowned in a widow's surf out in California,
or perhaps even phone the other friend,
an ex-priest, and listen to him say
the hands of the Church ache still
from the folly of trying to penknife astronomy:
I don't care . . . not now as I pull off my cowboy-
purple shirt and you laugh, ask if we shouldn't wait
until it's dark. But we're miles from eyes,
except Willie-the-family-goat who knows
nothing of nineteenth-century gestures of love,
the coupling of two old married lovers.
Later, you say it's as good as the day we did it
on the state park picnic table in dripping
gray weather. I say it's as good as the time
we made love in the brand-new stock tank
that August I had to mend a mess of barbwire fence.
Then, holding hands as we enter our home,
we don't even mind our four-year-old son
waking up and insisting on a glass of water,
a pee, and yet another shot at the mulberries.

1988

A western painting arrives.
The subdued mountain shadows
ease over a lone rider.
It is a license to keep
paying the bills:
a lullaby of cactus water
in a paperback outlaw novel.
Kate is curled on the couch
with me, a relic of the Golden
Nugget. We're giving fair
attention to breath and sweat,
fondling away an afternoon.
Age is a bother, a parent
with bad luck. The mark
is often over-shot,
and a life can become
a box of dog-eared postcards.
But the painting! Look at
the saddle beneath the rider,
how sunlight turns it
to chocolate. On this quiet
Las Vegas street, we touch
like two kids ditching school.

1989

The line at the video counter at Smith's
has to pass by a poster of a white bull,
with a parachute floating in a swimming pool
in the foreground. Maybe it's a film
about a rodeo bull who's spent
a glorious motel weekend. I once thought
to name my son Crazy Horse. We got
a daughter that time. I'm in another line
with a cartload of groceries. I hear
a few women behind me, but I don't turn
as they talk about renting a Madonna movie.
Then I turn around because they smell good:
four hookers in town from Pahrump—
pulsing pale makeup, much too grim-visaged
for showgirls. The redhead holds up
a copy of *Town and Country* and smirks at me.
"Honey, ya think I can make the cover of this here?"
The prettiest one has silver studs on a blouse
that only covers one shoulder and shows
a bit of nipple on one breast. She asks me
what I like. Ponies, all-night waitresses,
cattle out in Nebraska facing the Missouri River,
and hookers in line with ice cream and cigarettes.
"Sure," she says. "You a prudent type?"
Then she strokes a bare arm. And the girl
standing behind her says to no one,
"It's a tough road." A fourth girl,
let's call her Purple Camisole,
looks at the movie poster with the bull
and says, "The fucker looks rank,"
and right away I like her because
I like country girls.

1990

I'm eating chocolate cake at Cafe Michele
with TGL, an actress. Some very expensive cars
are parked illegally at the curb. We're talking
about a transvestite we know who finally got
the perfect breasts, high-tech Jell-O in sacks.
TGL's breasts are very real. Another car is parked
against the law, and I recognize the driver.
I tell TGL about the party last night, about
this guy who has just nodded to me and will spend
the afternoon selling bales of dope to other
men like himself. A former copter pilot in Vietnam.
I tell TGL, "The guy looks at her. She looks back.
He grabs his pecker, says 'Wanna do some blow?'
He strokes a statue of Bardot in the living room,
says, 'It never talks back.' And then he slaps it.
The girl follows him to the bathroom. The room
they left has 100 pictures of Marilyn Monroe
and one poster of a Face-of-the-'80s. Our host's
girlfriend, who is that face and body from the '80s,
says, 'We coulda gone to Paris last summer.'"
I tell TGL all this because she is the kind of woman
who needs to laugh in order to eat. TGL is laughing,
and her breasts blush above the low-cut dress.
TGL needs to catch a plane for L.A.
The cake is so good that I lick my plate clean.

1998

It's been one dusty August drought day,
and I ran three sagebrush and rattler miles,
too dogged by heat to dream old lovers.
Evening drew us to maps of the Great Basin,
names we've touched: Minersville, Panaca, Ely.
The carton of happiness, no larger than
a Stetson hat box, can burst in fire
so rapidly. Tonight we watch from the deck
after news of Sosa's 55th home run:
half a mile of grass is aflame
to the north, near Soap Lake,
and the smoke cloud is lit from beneath,
as if an iron fry pan ignited a burger.
More likely it's a boy and his cigarette.
Kate asks again about the baby rattler
in the freezer. Again I promise
it'll be rolling to Luke's school on the bus.
Kate says the fire is much closer than it seems,
maybe at Englehart's. Snatches of Springsteen
come from our house, so we can't hear the sirens
of the fire trucks coming from Moses Lake,
and I remember prizefighters in Las Vegas,
six-mile golf course runs, beautiful girls
in nothing but mink as they sulked to end
the roadwork of their men, maybe
"Glory Days" loud from a blaster over
the ninth hole at the Dunes. Brushfire love,
blonde pelvic surges in dark casino parking lots,
the dead too called upon with prayers to sleep:
tonight we turn off all our north-side lights,
for we know our neighbors are begging God
to stop the wind and grant darkness.

Envoy

We're outlaws, never caught or lost,
seekers on the desert. It doesn't pay to gum-up
love with questions. Last night in the kitchen's
courteous dark, Kate and I spoke of legends
of the West, names erased from wooden markers.
Whatever happened to High Noon or the expedition
against the Mormons? Kate's voice drifts
across the peach-colored sheet. Someone should
walk Cocoa-the-wolfhound. And I would vanish,
horseman refusing time's decay, if my eyes opened.
Her delicate breasts have fed our four children.
She brushes my arm as she counts the reasons
why it's the desperado who walks the dog.
But I'm only the high desert sky in a country song.